Written by
Andrew Fusek Peters
and Polly Peters
illustrated by
Finger Industries Ltd.

Alec
Mum
Roz
Maths
Nipper
Mae

Contents

Chapter 1
The Missing Keys

Mae was ready for school. Her brother, Alec, and her little sister, Roz, were ready, too. But Mum was rushing around. In fact, she was frantic.

"Where are the keys?" asked Mum, looking in the fridge. "I can't find them! We're going to be late!"

“I don’t want to be late,” cried Roz. “I’ve drawn a special picture for Mrs Jones. I want to show it to her and…”

“Give it a rest, Roz. Your whining is hurting my ears!” Alec moaned.

“But it’s a really good picture. I drew the whole street!”

Mae patted Roz’s shoulder. “Don’t worry. I’m sure the keys will turn up.” But Roz wasn’t listening.

"Mum!" Roz wailed. "It's my turn to feed our class pets, and I can't if we're late."

"That's enough!" cried Mum. "Everyone be quiet. I need to think."

Alec rolled his eyes. "Well, the keys haven't grown legs and walked off," he muttered.

"They haven't fallen in love with a key-ring and run away with it...

and our cat hasn't stolen them, because we don't have a cat. We have Nipper!"

"Alec, you're not being very helpful!" Mum sighed.

"I have an idea…" Mae began.

Mum interrupted. "I'll ring Mrs Gubbins over the road. Maybe she can drop you off at school while I keep searching for the keys."

Mae scowled, wondering if anyone would notice if she stood on her head – probably not this morning!

Chapter 2
Super Sleuth

Now everyone was rushing round – everyone except Mae. She tried again. "I have an idea ..."

No one was listening. Mae took a deep breath and yelled. "Can anybody out there hear me?"

Everyone stopped and stared.

"No need to shout, darling!" said Mum, who was punching numbers into the phone. "What is it? I'm really busy here."

"You should retrace your steps. When did you last see the keys?" asked Mae.

"You're not a TV detective, you know!" Alec teased.

"And as Mum said, *you're* not being very helpful!" hissed Mae.

"Mae has a point!" said Mum, cradling the phone. "I think… well… I drove Mae and Roz home yesterday afternoon. Yes, that was the last time I saw the keys."

"Good!" said Mae.

"Good?" echoed Roz. "How does that help?"

"Who lost the keys last time, Roz?" Mae asked.

Roz sucked her thumb and looked at the floor.

"Ah yes," said Alec. "Roz dropped them down the drain, remember?

It wasn't a super-sleuth detective who found them – just me and an old coat hanger, in the rain!"

Roz frowned. "I was only little!"

Mae sat down to think. She stared at Roz's picture on the table, but her thoughts were interrupted by a shout from Mum.

"Oh no! Is that the time?" asked Mum. "There's no answer from Mrs Gubbins. I'm going to miss the train and be late for my meeting today!"

Roz started sobbing, moaning about pictures and guinea pigs. Alec threw his bag on the floor.

"It's up to me!" Mae thought. Then she gasped. "I wonder ..."

Chapter 3
Big ideas

A picture was forming in Mae's mind. In the car on the way back from dance class yesterday, Roz had complained about needing the toilet. In fact, she had been so desperate that she couldn't sit still! She had fidgeted so much, that it looked like she was trying to practise her dance moves!

When they had arrived home, Mum was busy fishing out bits of shopping from the back of the car. But Roz had raced into the house to go to the toilet.

"Hmm," thought Mae. "Question number one!" she announced standing up. "Who was the first person through the front door yesterday afternoon?"

Mum looked at Roz. Roz looked at Mae. Mae looked back at Roz. Roz looked at the floor.

"Um, I don't know," mumbled Roz.

"I do," Mum said slowly.

Everyone turned to Roz and she turned red.

"I really needed the toilet!" said Roz.

"We know!" Mae carried on. "That's why Mum gave you the keys to open up. Where did you put them, Roz?"

"I don't know!" Roz stuck out her bottom lip. "It's not fair. I'm going to miss my turn to feed the pets."

Alec groaned. "Can I just go back to bed? Wake me up again tomorrow!"

But Mae had other ideas. "Come on. The keys have to be here somewhere!"

They searched in the kitchen cupboard, but all they found was a half-eaten sandwich.

They searched in the dog's basket, but all they found was one of Mum's shoes.

They searched under the stairs, but all they found was a smelly, old sock.

They even searched in the bath, but all they found was a big, hairy spider!

"Yuck!" Roz wrinkled her nose. "So much for your big ideas, big sister!"

Chapter 4
A Picture Clue

"I'll ring for a taxi!" Mum announced.

"Good idea," said Alec. "Can I wait outside? This kitchen is like a zoo!"

Roz pouted. "What do you mean?"

Alec smirked. "I mean, we've got a whining, Tantrum Monster in here!"

Roz made a face at him. "Mum! He's being mean!"

"Alec, leave your sister alone!" said Mum. "Now, where did I put that phone number?"

Mae was leaning on the kitchen table. Something caught her eye. "Aha!" she smiled, peering closely at Roz's drawing. "It's all in the picture!"

"Is it?" said Roz. "What? Like a secret code or something?"

"Not quite," said Mae.

Mum dropped her handbag. "Oh dear! Alec, be helpful. Look up the taxi company on the internet. I've lost the number."

"Everyone loses everything in this house," Alec muttered. "And I'm losing my mind."

Mae jumped up. "We don't need a taxi. I think I might have solved the case!"

"Really?" said Mum.

"You mean it might not be my fault?" Roz asked hopefully.

"I didn't say that, but if I work out where the keys are, will you tidy my room?" asked Mae.

"No way!" Roz shook her head.

"That's bribery!" said Mum. "But if you really have solved this mystery, you should be rewarded."

"OK," said Mae. "Here's what I think."

Chapter 5
Case Closed

Mae pointed at Roz's picture. She had drawn a window frame. Through the window, she had drawn the rooftops of all the houses on their street.

"This is the clue!" Mae announced.

The family gathered round.

"I don't see any keys!" said Roz.

"Of course you don't, but what did you do after you went to the toilet?"

"I drew my picture," said Roz. "What has that got to do with anything?"

"Where did you do it?" asked Mae.

"In the attic. I went straight up to look at the view."

"Exactly!" said Mae.

"If my detective work is right," said Mae, "then we need to look in the attic. Quickly, there's no time to lose!"

Everyone scrambled upstairs onto the landing. They stood at the bottom of the stairs that lead to the attic.

"Roz, you know what to do!" said Mum.

Roz was unusually quiet. She knew tantrums would not work now. She clambered up the stairs and disappeared from view.

A minute later, there was a squeal and the sound of running feet. Roz held out the jangling treasure. "The keys, I found them!" she said, excitedly.

"*I* found them!" said Mae. This time, everyone heard her.

"Am I in trouble?" Roz asked.

"Let's just say that you *will* be tidying Mae's room!" laughed Mum.

Alec shrugged. "I suppose you're the smart-alec today, Mae."

Mum looked at her watch. "Come on everyone. Class pets to feed. Trains to catch. Let's go!"

Mae decided to try her luck. "Mum, can we go swimming after school and have hot chocolate afterwards?"

How could Mum say no to the fabulous Super Sleuth?